Solar System Explorers

Neptune

Written by
E.C. Andrews

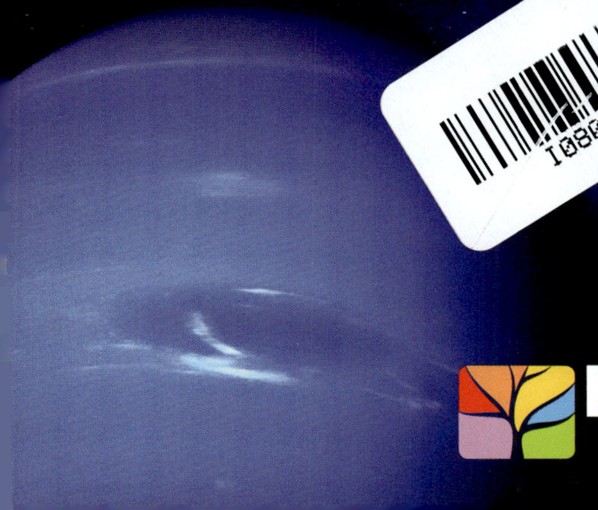

KidHaven
PUBLISHING

Published in 2026 by
KidHaven Publishing, an Imprint of
Greenhaven Publishing, LLC
2544 Clinton St., Buffalo, NY 14224

Written by: E.C. Andrews
Edited by: Noah Leatherland
Designed by: Amelia Harris

Cataloging-in-Publication Data
Names: Andrews, E.C.
Title: Neptune / E.C. Andrews.
Description: Buffalo, NY : Kidhaven Publishing, 2026. | Series: Solar System Explorers | Includes glossary and index
Identifiers: ISBN 9781534549852 (pbk) | ISBN 9781534549869 (library bound) | ISBN 9781534549876 (ebook)
Subjects: LCSH: Neptune (Planet)—Juvenile Literature
Classification: LCC QB691 A53 2026 | DDC 523.48--dc25

Manufactured in the United States of America

CPSIA compliance information: Batch #CSKH26
For further information contact Greenhaven Publishing LLC at 1-844-317-7404.

Please visit our website, www.greenhavenpublishing.com.
For a free color catalog of all our high-quality books, call toll free 1-844-317-7404 or fax 1-844-317-7405.

Find us on

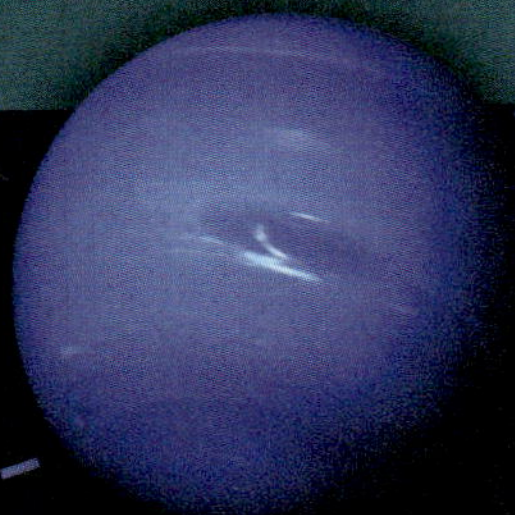

Image Credits

Images are courtesy of Shutterstock.com. With thanks to Getty Images, Thinkstock Photo and iStockphoto. Cover – 19 STUDIO, AspctStyle, andreysharonov, M.Aurelius. Recurring Images – thomas eder, YummyBuum, Sabelskaya. 4–5 – 24K-Production, Withan Tor. 6–7 – bilgeari, Vadim Sadovski. 8–9 – Nemes Laszlo, Vadim Sadovski. 10–11 – AspctStyle. 12–13 – Vadim Sadovski, buradaki, NASA/JPL, Public domain, via Wikimedia Commons. 14–15 – newelle, buradaki, Artsiom P, NASA, Public domain, via Wikimedia Commons. 16–17 – Vlad Ra27, buradaki, Vadim Sadovski. 18–19 – Vadim Sadovski, NASA/JPL, CC BY 4.0, via Wikimedia Commons. 20–21 – carlosramos1946, Zwiebackesser, Artsiom P. 22–23 – Vadim Sadovski.

Contents

Words that look like this can be found in the glossary on page 24.

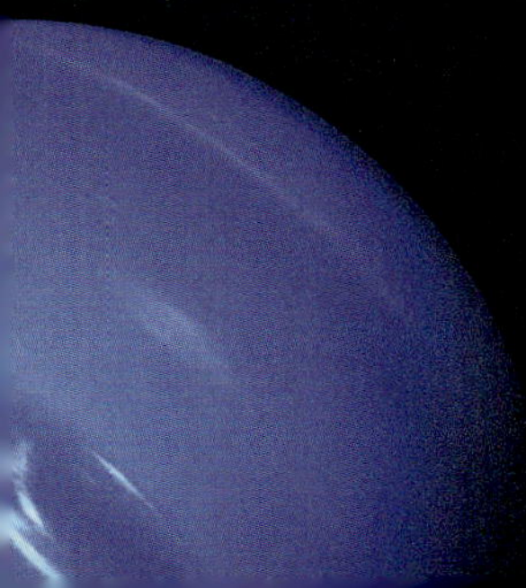

Let's Explore!

The solar system is home to planets and other objects that **orbit** a star called the sun. It is a big place, but the solar system explorers are up for the challenge.

Today, our space rocket is blasting off to one of the farthest corners of the solar system. We are on a mission to explore the planet Neptune. Wrap up warm, explorers, because this is a chilly one!

Where Is Neptune?

Every planet in the solar system orbits the sun at a different distance. If we were to line them up in order, it would look something like this:

As you can see, Neptune is the farthest planet from the sun. It is around 2.8 billion miles (4.5 billion km) away. Neptune does not get much sunlight. It is very dark and very cold.

Neptune can only be seen from Earth with a telescope.

Round and Round

Earth takes around 365 days to orbit the sun. This is how humans measure one year. However, it takes Neptune 60,190 days to orbit the sun. That is almost 165 years on Earth.

Neptune's orbit takes so long because of how far away it is.

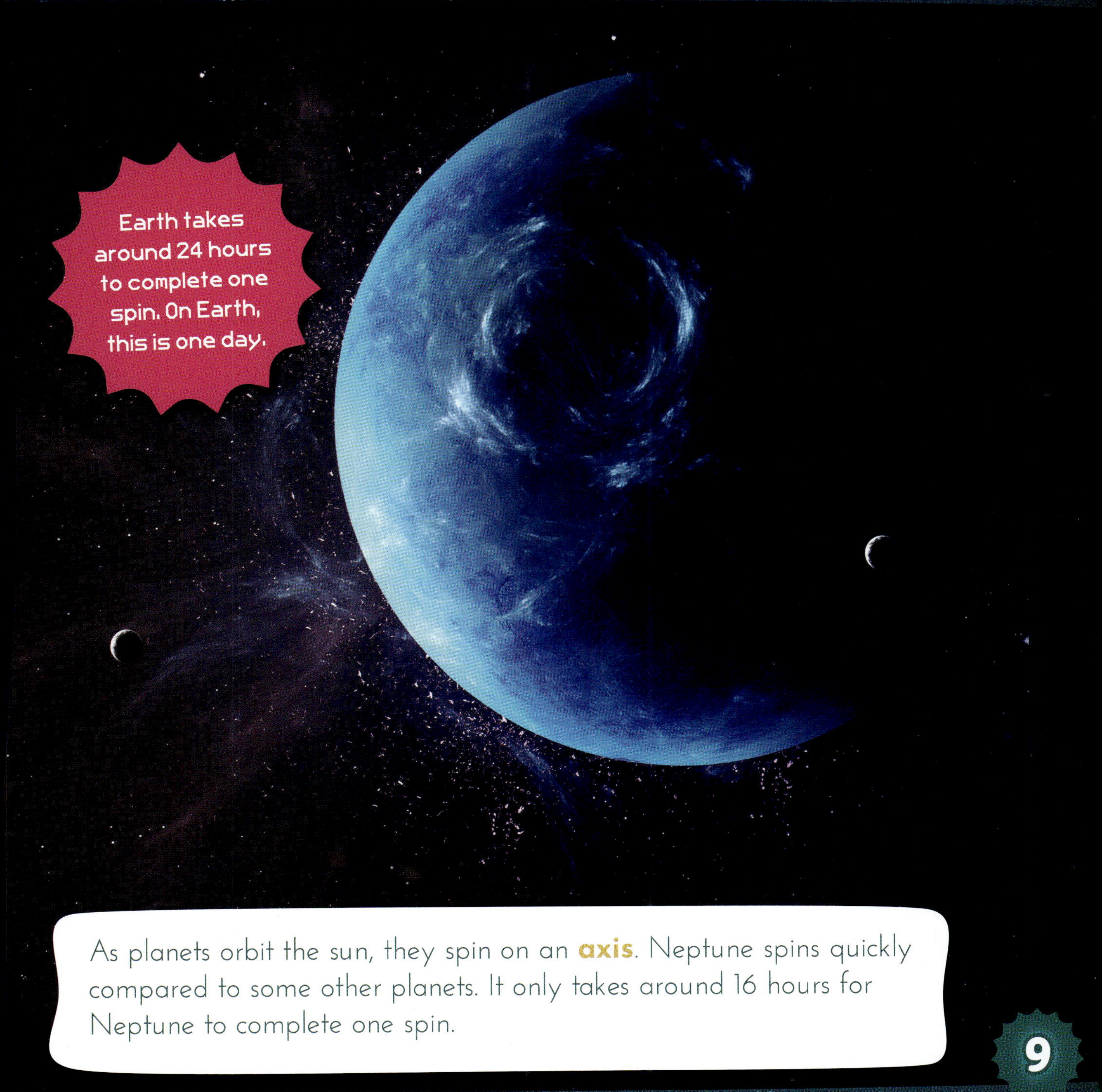

Earth takes around 24 hours to complete one spin. On Earth, this is one day.

As planets orbit the sun, they spin on an **axis**. Neptune spins quickly compared to some other planets. It only takes around 16 hours for Neptune to complete one spin.

Planet Profile

Here are some notes on Neptune that we have in our database.

Temperature

Neptune is about minus 330 degrees Fahrenheit (-200°C).

Water freezes at 32°F (0°C).

Size

- Around: 96,129 miles (154,704 km)
- Across: 30,775 miles (49,528 km)

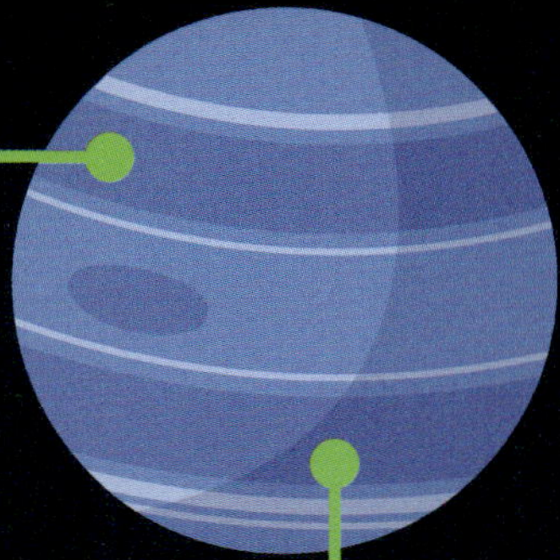

Water boils at 212°F (100° C).

What Is Neptune Made Of?

Neptune is a type of planet called an ice giant. It is covered in thick fog made of water and **gases** such as ammonia and methane. Neptune has six rings made of icy dust.

The dust that makes up the rings is pulled in by Neptune's **gravity**.

Neptune is thought to have four layers.

Upper Atmosphere

Neptune's upper **atmosphere** is a layer of ice and water.

Mantle

Neptune's mantle is a huge ocean of water, ammonia, and ice.

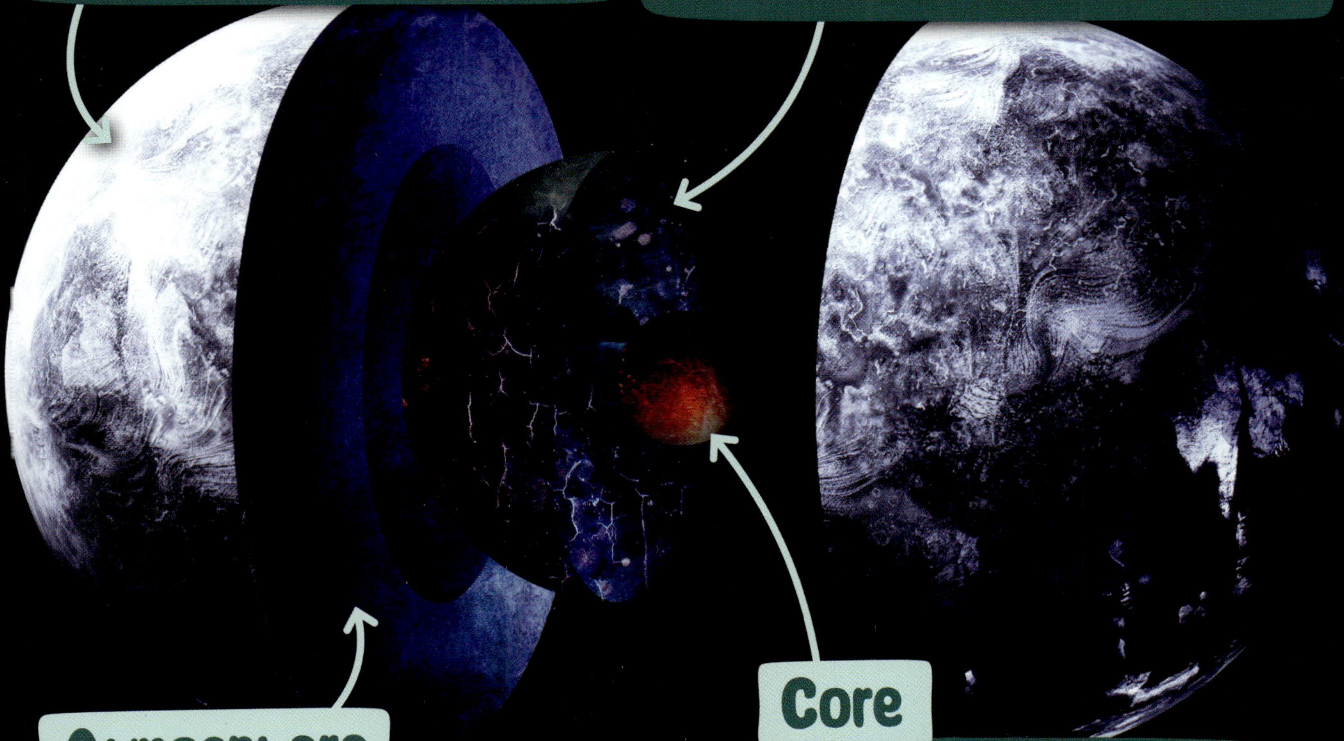

Atmosphere

The rest of Neptune's atmosphere is full of gases such as hydrogen, helium, and methane.

Core

Neptune's core is a freezing, Earth-sized ball of solid rock and ice.

Watching the Weather

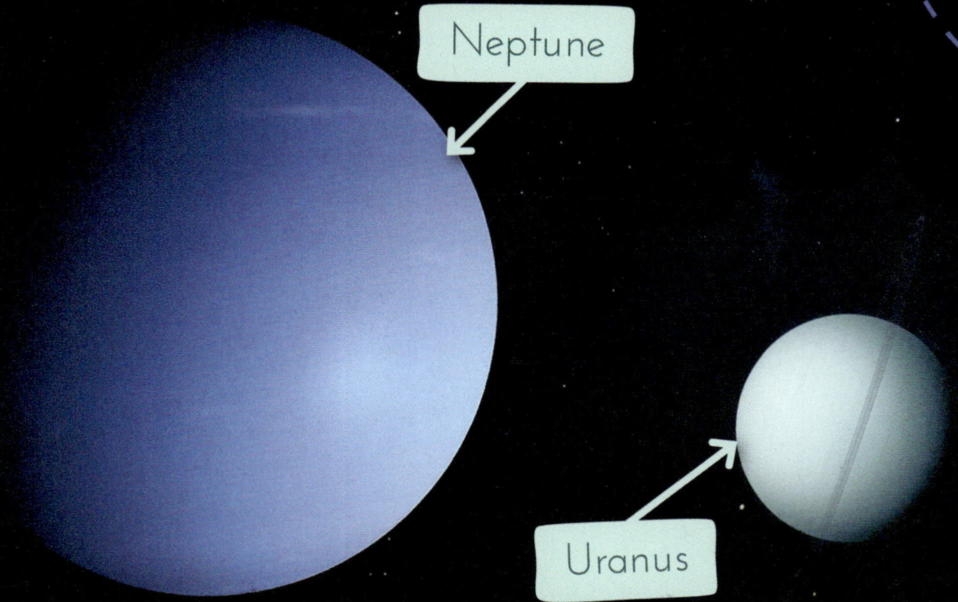

Even though it is the farthest planet from the sun, Neptune is not the coldest planet in the solar system. The coldest planet in the solar system is Neptune's neighbor and fellow ice giant, Uranus.

Neptune is still a very chilly place, of course. It is also very windy. The wind on Neptune can reach up to 1,250 miles (2,000 km) an hour. These are the strongest winds in the entire solar system.

Is There Life on Neptune?

A planet that things can live on is called a habitable planet. There are no living things on Neptune that we know of. Neptune will probably not be habitable anytime soon.

Firstly, Neptune is far too cold for life as we know it to live there. There is also no oxygen. Living things need oxygen to stay alive.

Spot the Satellites

Something that orbits a bigger object is called a satellite. Some satellites are made by humans. Other satellites are made of rocks or other materials from space. These are **natural** satellites.

Moons are natural satellites. Neptune has 16 known moons.

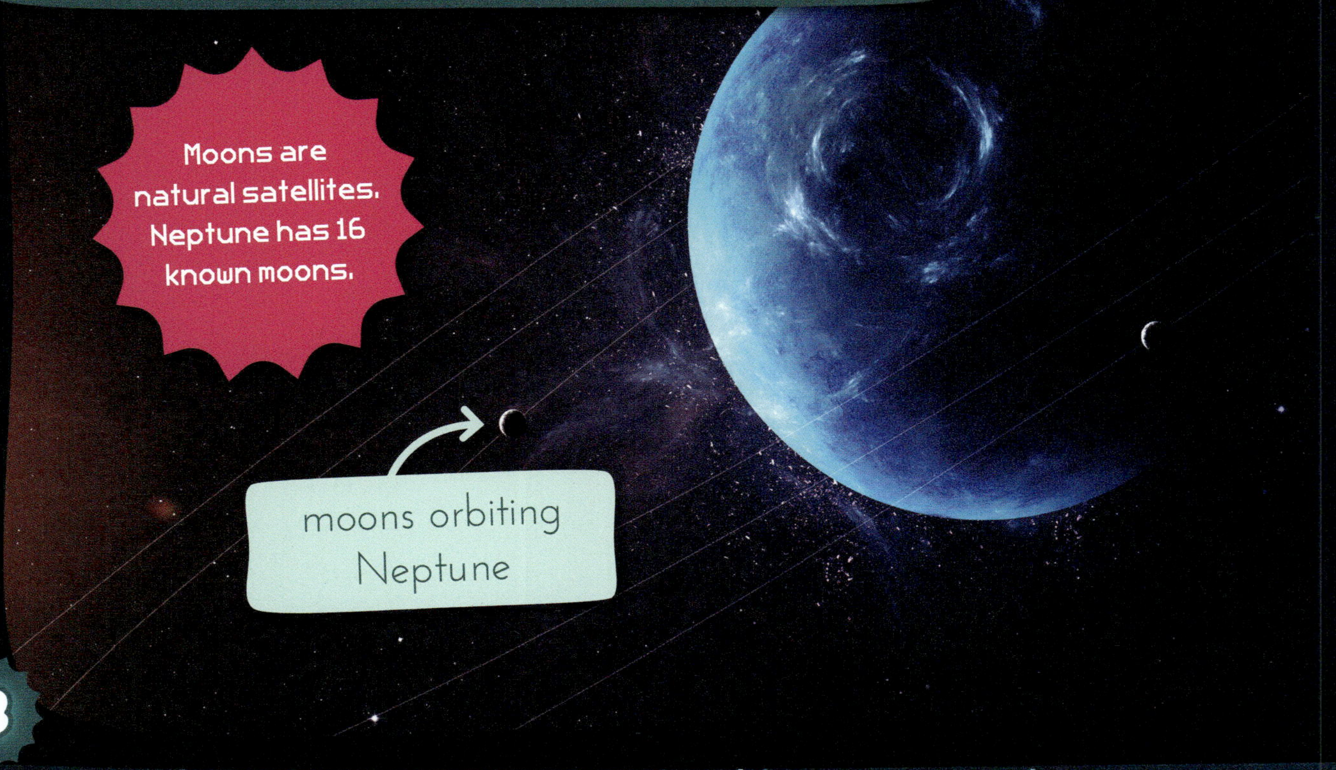

moons orbiting Neptune

Triton is the largest of Neptune's moons. Triton orbits Neptune in the opposite direction to the way Neptune spins. This is called a retrograde orbit. Triton is the only large moon in the solar system with a retrograde orbit.

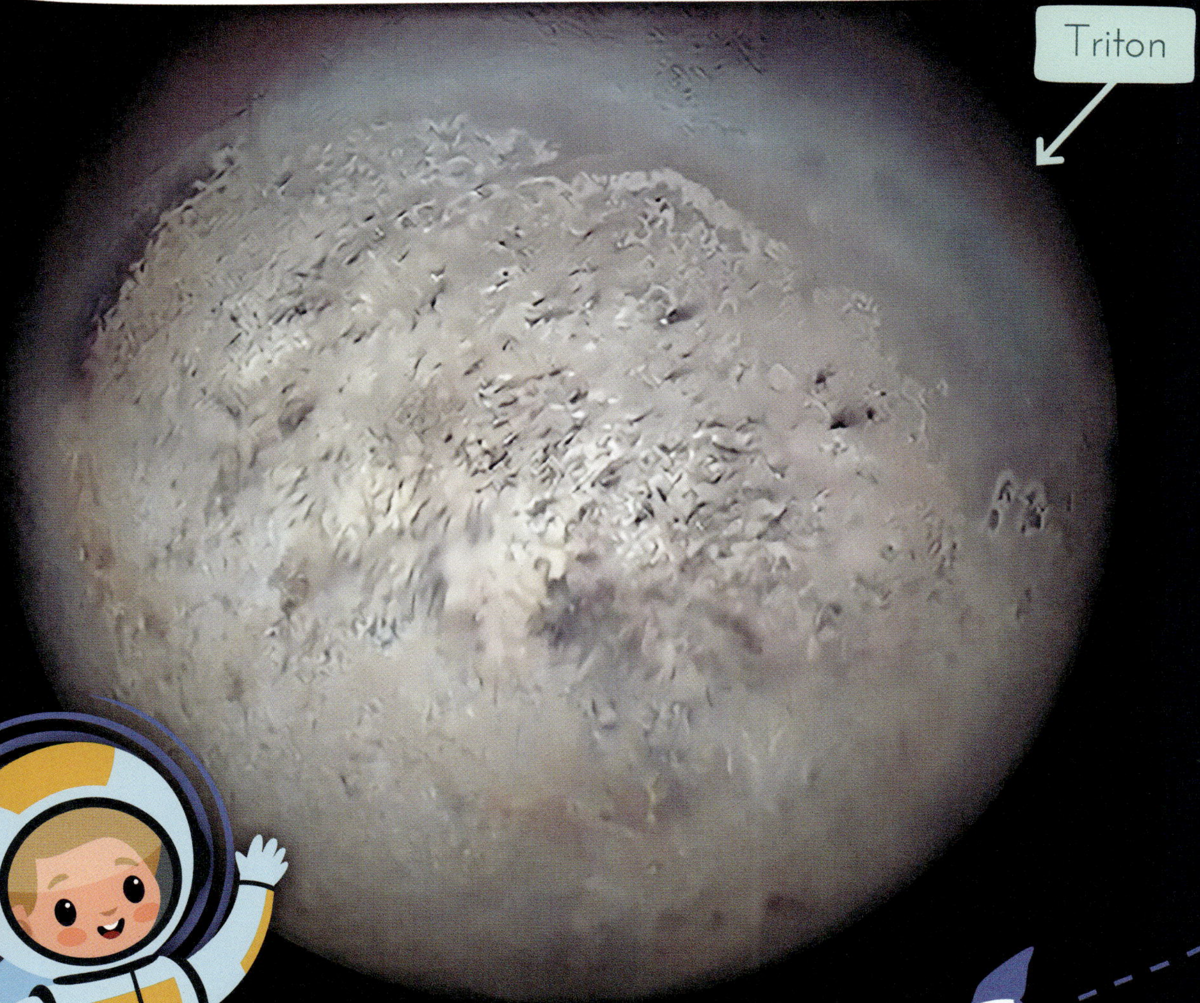

Why Is Neptune Blue?

You may have noticed its beautiful blue color. Neptune is this color because of a gas called methane. The methane in Neptune's atmosphere **absorbs** red light, while the blue light is **reflected** into space.

Neptune was named after the **ancient** Roman god of the sea because of its blue color. Neptune was a good name as humans later discovered the planet is covered in ice and water.

a statue of Neptune

More to Explore

Exploring this distant planet was always going to be a challenge. But what a fascinating mission it has been. We have learned so much about this icy planet. What an incredible place.

However, it is time to wave goodbye to the planet Neptune. There are lots of other things in the solar system waiting to be explored. Hopefully our next mission is somewhere warmer!

Glossary

absorbs	takes in or soaks something up
ancient	belonging to the very distant past
atmosphere	the mixture of gases that makes up the air and surrounds a planet
axis	an imaginary line that something turns on
degrees	measuring units used to explain how hot or cold something is
gases	things that are like air, which fill any space available
gravity	the force that pulls everything downward toward the center of large objects in space
natural	found in nature and not made by people
orbit	move around a star or planet in a curved path
reflected	to have bounced off

Index